bear creek haiku anthology

the poets of bear creek

Copyright © 2013 ayaz daryl nielsen
All rights reserved.
ISBN:1480001821
ISBN-13:978-1480001824

for the poets and their poetry which have
found (and will continue to find) a home upon
the pages of bear creek haiku

with deepest appreciation
ayaz daryl nielsen

poets of bear creek haiku...

Kelley Jean White

After thirty years of practice in inner-city Philadelphia Kelley White is very pleased to have returned to practice at a rural health center in New Hampshire, her home state. She has been sobered to find that rural poverty hurts as much as urban poverty.

Oh, poor dry stiff moth,
i sweep you up with day's dust--
flutter up, fly free!

I was the tree.
I sang windfall and night,
swallowed moonlight, and grew.

I imagined a
small black cat. He was there when
I opened the door.

unpierced ears
unlike all the others
virgin virgin

1

on hold: roar
of the emergency room
in the background

Downstairs — Zen typing:
unheard until I climb the stairs —
raindrops on the roof.

I wanted
          to be
      a clear
cold stream:
      that you
    might drink
        and be
      refreshed

                          voiceless
                          I might have learned
                          to listen

Margaret D. McGee

When I feel grounded in creation and connected through the stories and places of my life, I am better able to live authentically. As a writer and teacher, I work with various practices of attention and mindfulness to develop a sense of connection and being at home in the cosmos. I'm the author of Haiku - The Sacred Art and Sacred Attention, both published by Sky-Light Paths. My first book, Stumbling Toward God, was published by Innisfree Press. My web site, "In the Courtyard" at inthecourtyard.com, is the home of online classes, retreats, and other resources that celebrate mindful practices leading to authentic life, as well as a reservoir of original reflections, meditations, prayers, and poetry.

harvest moon
another layer of duct tape
on the garden gloves

daybreak
a slug beats me
to the strawberry

a mushroom caps
the old fence post
I will be what I will be

night balancing day
across the withered fence, mist clings
to withered fields

> stove smoke
> circles up; a paisley scarf
> rests beside the ax

leaf buds
on the prickly rose. . .
mom's birthday call

> camp tea
> flames die to ember
> while ravens mutter

60th birthday--
dirt under my fingernails
sap rising in my veins

Diane Webster

People ask how I can persist submitting when I receive more rejections than acceptances. People ask if I get paid. People ask if they've heard of the magazines I get published in. People don't understand why I still write. Like all of us I write because I can't not write. I see something interesting or maybe even ordinary, and it tickles my imagination. I may toy with it for weeks or I may scramble for paper right then because some ideas poof away with only a residual wisp that I had a great thought. I tell people I started writing as soon as I learned how to write. That's what my core person is. A writer. Using my imagination and perspective to see something different. Sometimes people don't get it or shake their heads. Like watching clouds. I may see a whole battle of dragons and knights clashing while others wonder why I even notice clouds. They're just clouds, to them. Writing poetry, I try to scratch those people's imaginations. If it feels like barbed wire across their backs; if it feels like a single spiderweb strand caressing their cheeks; if it feels like a butterfly navigating arm hairs, then I've made someone hesitate, for a moment.

Rows of frosted trees sparkle –
white-haired ladies
wait in bus line

        After the hail storm
        rose bud found on the ground
        blooms in a glass

STUMP GROWTH

Each shelf of mushroom
grows over the lower
like ledges of granite
in a waterfall blurring
start to finish
in a cascading wash
of perpetual movement. . .
in mushroom speed
of course.

PASSING PETRIFIES

We walk barefoot
in mud hoping
our passing
petrifies
in drying sun
like two dinosaurs
out for a stroll.

on coffee-colored mountain
I fall asleep

Pat Prine

Retired, after working for many years in a community college library, I live in a suburb of Chicago with my husband Dave and our two cats. I have been writing poetry for many years, experimenting in many forms, but in the last few years I have narrowed it down to short forms – haiku, cinquain, and recently tanka. My favorite form of poetry is now haiku. To write a good haiku is a joy.

standing guard
in the children's playground
a green rhinoceros

Happy Birthday!
Dad's old flannel jacket
still hanging in the closet

IN PRAISE OF FAILURE

The great thing about failure
is you don't have to top it
Expectations plunge, eyes are averted
In fact, no one is even watching anymore.
A curious freedom, a welcome release.
You no longer even have to try.

ARGUMENT

Acid-venom-verbal lacerations preside
over the breakfast table
Words slam against the wall, skate across the
ceiling
crash into the door
And can never be retrieved.

incessant chattering
a convention of squirrels
in my front yard

a piece of driftwood
over the mantel piece
the fire is out

Spring rain
gently falling
turning grass green, prodding
tree buds to open, birds to nest.
New life.

George Held
is a poet, writer, and haikuist, who greatly admires Basho.

A touch of chill
a hint of warm –
   April Fool's

            Aging uniforms
            parading on main street –
            Memorial Day

Clover displacing
grass on the year –
   lucky yard

            Petroleum Blues

            We got Oil in the marshes
            We got Oil in the tide pools

            We got Oil in the crawdads
            We got Oil on the beaches

            We got Oil in our future
            A-throttlin' Mother Nature

            We got them 'ol Petroleum --
            I said -- them 'ol Petroleum Blues

Hack Poet

For Dave Church

You drove whenever –
Nights, holidays, hurricanes –
Your notebook beside you
To receive a new idea
For poem or story whenever
It came to you

Till last Thanksgiving, when
Your hack came to a stop
With your last heart-thump.
Every passenger
In the small press
Mourns your loss.

        About life,
           about death,
        make no fuss

    5 AM
  radio signal fading
    bird song

Dorothy McLaughlin

Dorothy McLaughlin spent her first twenty-six years in Massachusetts. She attended Bridgewater State Teachers College where she majored in history and education and minored in French. She taught social studies in Springfield, Massachusetts, married her husband Jim, and they eventually moved to Somerset, New Jersey, with daughter Theresa and son Thomas. She and Jim recently celebrated their Fiftieth anniversary. Dorothy has been writing for over thirty years, articles, essays, free verse, haiku and tanka. She was facilitator of a haiku workshop at Osher Lifelong Learning Institute at Rutgers University, and she and Pat Laster published their haiku collection "Connecting Our Houses". She is a member of the Haiku Society of America and the Tanka Society of America and enjoys working with two tanka workshops, Tanka Twists, and, the New York Tanka Workshop. Twice nominated for a Pushcart Prize, she's making slow progress in putting together a book of her poems.

the sound of the wind
   clearing a path for itself
      through the trees
(from bear creek haiku #1, 1991)

                    my shadow
                    on the mirror
                    in the mirror

left in the shop
the dress that didn't fit
her budget

overcast morning
the world
without blue

before the sun
before the bird
alarm clock

family reunion
fingerprints and memories
don't match

evening peace vigil
candle flames flicker
touched by our prayers

George Matey

George Matey is an advertising Creative Director who is always grateful to be included in bear creek haiku. I enjoy reading the variety of poetry from so many poets. I always look forward to my favorites - Carl Mayfield, Dorothy Mc-Laughlin, Jane Stewart and Kelley Jean White. Dorothy, Jane, Kelley and I go back all the way to 2005 and the late lamented Haiku Headlines out of L.A. In fact, there was a bio of Kelley Jean White that year which mentioned bear creek haiku, and created my interest in this publication.

Child at a petting zoo.
A tiny hand strokes my arm.

Thoughts--
Butterflies seeking
the amber of memory.

Tinkling temple bells.
Peeing in a toilet.

wiping up spilled sherry,
the wooden sideboard
hiccups.

13

Green.
Yellow.
Red.
Autumn is not a sudden stop.

sign language
reflected in a store window.
deaf man
talking to himself.

early morning phone call
company is downsizing
cut before shaving

Thoughts--
Butterflies seeking
the amber of memory.

Jane Stuart

I - I have a PhD - didn't know what a cell phone was - I said "certainly not" to someone - I thought he meant jail. It's a family house, an old log cabin - rewiring was done, but I didn't get hooked up - I learned later that I had two telephone numbers - no, just one - and that one had been changed - I had none. But I did not want to argue with anyone about having email or my getting on internet or about my being able to go online. I don't know how to use and choose, I don't know how to get rid of a virus, so I work slowly and mostly by longhand. I can write, setup, store (save) and print with some organization, but I use index cards, too. It's all hard copy and snail mail.

park concert's final note -
a red Frisbee
thumps the bass drum

A rin-tinny day
Rusty memories
Caught in gusts of wind

early morning wind
whispering through meadow grass
an ancient love song

A lonely flute played
in a castle by the sea
many years ago

A whispering wind
Wakes the owl and warns the hawk
Snow is on the moon

Floating under rocks
a broken oar and tattered sail
grabbing at the sea

                    Morning follows night
                    moon falls into paradise
                    listen to the sun.

Alone, on the beach
our nets fill with starry night
driftwood and seashells

Judith Partin-Nielsen

Following a trail of words, mountains, spirit and tears, this writer, mother, wife and eventually psychoanalyst left Texas for Colorado in 1985. The land of the Arapahoe welcomed me and called me by name. The love of poetry, poet and high mountain valleys has warmed my heart and made my home. Freud said "everywhere I go, the poet has gone before me." May we keep following those footsteps on our paths thru the worlds. This contributor teaches contemplative psychotherapy at Naropa University, practices psychoanalysis and writes poetry.

Tibet Is a Country
young monk's red
and saffron robes
dissolving into flame
the intersection of
faith, courage and despair

Outside the rug shop
Tibetan flag flutters
Mourning the death
of the "land of snows"

Winter Woman

skin of golden ash
mystery of face
abstracted in beauty
loosened chignon of promise
graceful ellipses of waist, widening to
hips opening like
the mouth of a river
giving birth to the world

Losing Texas #1

Rolling slowly across the
grey tarmac, sunset –
past glimpses of green Pine,
grazing cows, barbed-wire fences
the ache of leaving
blazing yellow orb
in blood-streaked skies
the plane ascends

Candi Cooper-Towler

was born in Boulder City, Nevada and now lives in Boulder County, Colorado. She shares her life with her novelist husband, two black cats, a dog and a horse. Hobbies beyond haiku include hiking, horseback archery, dog agility, and video gaming. Her main goals in life are to own a house with a turret, and get daydreaming accepted as an Olympic sport.

bathroom sink
overflowing
sleeping cat

bloody knuckles
but the toilet works

shopping
none of my scribbles
match the wine labels

wind in the pine —
blessed silence
after the grocery store

the summer night flavors
moon in my teacup

I want to tell you
this year
I kept my roses alive

          clandestine meeting
          kisses smell like gasoline

I don't want to go anywhere
well maybe
ice cream

cat inside
a paper bag
cat on top

herd of dry leaves
clattering by

John Grey

Australian born poet, playwright, musician, Providence, RI resident since late seventies. Works as financial systems analyst. Has been published in numerous magazines including Weird Tales, Christian Science Monitor, Agni, Poet Lore, and, Journal Of The American Medical Association as well as the horror anthology "What Fears Become", work in Poem, Prism International and the Potomac Review. Has had plays produced in Los Angeles and off-off Broadway in New York. Winner of Rhysling Award for short genre poetry in 1999.

second hand store
busy hands try on gloves
old hands wore

catch and release
mountain stream
singles bar

cold morning
frog tongue
licks the air

late night sidewalk
cast off wrappers
flapping fences

dying parlor fire
soft cackle glowing coals
low flame of sleep

swimmer
humanizes
ocean

no moon
dark river
travels by sound

wild waves
feeding pelicans
splash dance

Dennis Saleh

Born in Chicago, raised and educated in California and Arizona, in a psychology graduate PhD program with a Clinical Internship from the National Institute of Mental Health, he changed course and has an MFA in Creative Writing. For several years, he lectured at the University of California and California State University campuses. Saleh's poetry, prose and artwork appear in US publications and abroad, he is the author of several poetry books. He has edited an anthology of contemporary American poetry "Just What the Country Needs, Another Poetry Anthology". Editor and publisher of Comma Books, he has two books in co-imprint editions: Rock Art: The Golden Age of Record Album Covers (Comma/Ballantine Books) and Science Fiction Gold: Film Classics of the 50s (Comma/ McGraw Hill). He also has written an as yet unpublished novel, "Pomegranate", about Oscar Wilde's 1882 US lecture tour. Three enduring interests of Saleh's are Outer Space, Ancient Egypt and the Rolling Stones. He and his wife, Michele, gave a skull-encrusted ring to Keith Richards, who kissed Michele on the cheek and said "thank you, Darlin'." Two of Saleh's favorite words are 'ineluctable" and "more." He is known for never taking no an answer.

Mirror

Sorrow

so perfect

it brings a smile

(Dennis Saleh, continued)

Japanese
garden
snow
falls in
perfect
time

Koan
Two words
why more

Decor
Flamingo,
interrogative
of the lawn
shrill pink
question
mark,
unsettled
day-long
inquiry.

Noel Sloboda

lives on a lot with close to one hundred mature trees. He writes his best poetry during fall while moving this year's leaves. Sloboda also draws inspiration from his three dogs, who constantly draw him out of his head into the wild.

memory of you
strutting in heels
across decades

    feral cats
    insinuating shadows
    between tombstones

        dorm windows
        blazing before sunrise –
        exam day

    conductor
    wildly gesticulating
    good intentions

chalk on the blackboard
always the same painful squeal
first day back

fall showers,
acting unpredictable -
outdoor rehearsal

furious growling
Saturday at six a.m.
the neighbor's mower

dented mailbox
where the owl stopped
so many feathers

after hail
dimples all around the lot
not a single smile

an icy field
one cow chewing
silence

Stephanie Hiteshew

Stephanie resides in Ellicot City, Maryland, where she writes poetry, delves into photography, and writes within a circle of literary friends. She has published in ABBEY, The Aurorean, and Trajectory. Stephanie continues to write and read poetry while coping with four neurological involuntary movement disorders. She is treated by Specialists on a regular basis, taking with her a pen and paper whenever she goes. Despite some of the content of her poetry, it is where Stephanie finds her peace and her escape from the lifelong disorders she has to deal with.

Lonely Evening

The streets echo,
late into a
lonely evening,
my name.

Old Song

Old song, sing
me to sleep –
Rock me like
the ocean –
Cradle me like
the wind.

Emerald Eyes
She stole the view
with her
emerald eyes -
away from the fields,
away from the stars.

It Can't Be
Admiring
the view.
Leaves fall
upon my face.
Could it be?
No.
It can't be love.

Oh
rose
that blew
apart

p l wick

Over four decades of writing p. l. wick has been a contributor to numerous publications including noted youth and organization periodicals, newspaper columns, literary journals, grassroots publications, poetry reviews — even outlaw biker magazines. One award recognized book and a dozen chapbooks are among his credits. wick's introspection: "a versifier, perhaps. A poet, only on my cold gray granite slab."

let us doze together
and journey tomorrow
midst butterscotch pine

Descent

Soon

no one

old enough

to be my

parent

Save

the moon

collar turned against
snow dusted
late autumn winds
Memories
   slip from my pockets,
so many,
   dry yellow
leaves
blowing away to dance
with those gypsy
   days of summer

Shoe-gooed, hot glued,
duct taped and crudely
home-stitched,
the uppers of my
faithful hiking boots
are still serviceable.
However, the soles
have finally said,
enough.

Cathy Porter

Cathy Porter's poetry has appeared in Plainsongs, Pegasus, Art:Mag and other journals. Her chapbook "A Life in The Day" is available from Finishing Line Press and she also has two self-published chapbooks available. She lives in Omaha, Nebraska, and can be reached at cclon@q.com.

crows on bare branches
night filling
up with dark

TO DREAM OF TRAINS

Railroad tracks divide
the have-nots
and the have-even-less.
At night, you can hear
a lone whistle, mixed with footsteps.
Some walk these tracks
with dreams of hopping a train
to anywhere town;
others sit and pray
for a direct hit.

(Cathy Porter, continued)

ACOUSTIC MOON

In the still, our notes
as one: we wander unafraid,
houses folded and silent –
Each pause filled, we play
in the reflections, the sweetest sounds,
under an acoustic moon

HAIRSTYLES

She lets her guard down
as her hair falls upon bare shoulders;
his touch erasing the past.

In the morning,
she puts her hair up with her guard,
heads out the door to work,
wondering if he likes her hair up or down.

I never new that
I could put words in your mouth
by removing your foot

Martha Christina

Born and raised in Indiana, Martha Christina has lived for many years in Rhode Island, which is actually shaped a bit like Indiana. She is known among family and friends as a procrastinator, and though she enjoys reading the notes of others, she has never written a contributor's note that pleased her.

A SEVEN CARROT CHORUS

Chop. Chop. Chop. Chop.
Chop. Chop. Chop.
Seven bright exclamation points
reduced to periods.

IN GRANDMOTHER'S KITCHEN

A torn web stretches
from the corner of the sideboard
to the opened west window.
Trapped there: a silver hair.

JUST OFF THE FREE-WAY

mockingbird
scat singing
over horns

SCATTERED

thoughts
like coins
thrown
on cold linoleum

AT THE LIBRARY

In the children's room
I found
a safe place,
made of these books
a new family.

FAITH

Again rain is forecast,
and again it rains.
Again the cat sits
in the south window,
sure of tomorrow's predicted sun.

Seren Fargo

Seren Fargo, once (and still wishing to be) a wildlife researcher with the U.S. Forest Service, now writes poetry, particularly Japanese-form. She finds this poetry form best satisfies both her creative side and her scientific side. In 2009, she founded the Bellingham Haiku Group, which she currently coordinates (https://sites.google.com/site/bellinghamhaikugroup/home). Her work has won several awards and been published in many journals in the United States and internationally. Her writing largely reflects two major aspects of her life: her passion for the natural world and her struggles with chronic illness and loss, often in tandem with nature. Seren also loves photography and hopes to one day pursue presenting her work in shows and galleries. She lives in a rural setting in the Pacific Northwest with her three cats, Badger, Princess Kita, and 20-year-old Neptune.

ritual
opening of window coverings
each day
the leaves
a shade yellower

paws over whiskers
        hands over harp strings

His toothbrush
in the glass next to mine
his unused.

Whoosh! Whoosh!
rushing wind
looking up to see
a mobiling play of
crows in a downdraft

No Children

Without the next generation,
the finality of death is erasure.

So I will continue to write in ink.

backpedaling
as I head
        down
            the hill
where I grew up

Peggy Dugan French

Peggy Dugan French is a California girl with Minnesota roots, she savors a walk on the beach or a stroll around a farm in equal measure. She loves cats, cows, flowers, and vacationing in Big Sur. She will always buy the biggest Christmas tree that will fit into her house. She is married to her soul mate and they have shared a long and varied road together. She has worn many hats over the years, but being a Mom has been one of her greatest adventures, her kids think she's the cats meow and this makes her smile. She has also been the Office Manager for her husband's business, Director's Assistant at her daughter's dance studio, homework monitor, daughter, sister, friend and the Editor of Shemom since 1997. Her kids have now flown the nest and although she does miss the hum of a full house, she is enjoying the next leg of her journey. One of her greatest pleasures is to sit around a dinner table with her family sharing food, wine, music and conversation. She is delighted to be part of this anthology and share the page with the fine writers that Daryl has brought together. Thanks for the opportunity.

curious cow
stares me down
love at first sight

Maybe I should consider myself lucky.
yes
I'm glad you didn't stay
leaving me with a lifetime
of dirty dishes

          sugar plums
          dressed in pink
          the journey begins

          first solo
             pride
          in every step

          first tutu
            smiles
          ear to ear

          hours upon hours
          finally
          a dancer

   farm kittens
   the city kids
   fuss over each one

John Constantine Mastor

lives in Seattle with his wife Linda and two rambunctious felines, Cali and Gibbs. Has had short stories, articles and poetry published, including four chapbooks of poetry in the 1990's, the last being Studio Portrait (1999 The Plowman). Has had poetry and haiku published in Bellowing Ark, Pot-pourri, Silver Wings, Haiku Hippodrome, The Oak, The Poet's Ark and many more. Enjoys traveling, bowling, reading, coin and postcard collecting and attending sporting events.

Dying is an Art
I am perfecting every day.

Rear View

Traveling light –
I keep my past
out of sight.

Blue mood,
a cloud-like vapor,
misty eyes.

last chance
always
the hardest to grasp.

39

Reeling in salmon
Puget Sound waters
fishing for poems.

Fishing expedition
retrieving poems
from cold storage

Midwestern summer
humidity rising
missing Seattle.

Snow flakes fall . . .
icy streets: somewhere
a baby sleeps.

Ends.
What all good things
come to.

James B Peters

James B Peters is retired. He became interested in poetry and short stories while earning a B. A. in English. His poems have appeared in Capper's, Kentucky Living, Haiku Head-lines, Gusts, bear creek haiku along with local Tennessee venues.

Just a kiss hello
a long hug to let her know
You still love her so

In summer heat
a five year old,
a garden hose

a small stream trickles
over layers of worn stone
the sound of old tunes

Through a veil
Of wind blown snow
An old barn,
With its doors ajar

High on the mountains
Among the snowflakes
Only wind complains

    Just Americans
    Those who hold the corvette dream
    Those who build the car.

    As the sun rises
    the clocks chime to the badges
    of corvette builders

    end of vette summer
    a Labor Day homecoming
    race on the blacktop

    Just a red corvette
    On a winding country road
    South Kentucky pride

Everything is damp
In the early morning fog
Even the chickens

42

Dennis Rhodes

Dennis Rhodes is author of "Spiritual Pizza and Other Poems" and "Entering Dennis"

I flirted with death a year ago
(I think it was a sin)
Lucky for me I'm not the type
he has an interest in.

Too light to be night,
much too dark to be daytime:
dawn rules its own realms.

Saw bumper sticker
LIFE IS SHORT. PLAY WITH YOUR DOG.
Seems like good advice.

> Being misguided
> by your own conscience
> is far better
> than being misguided
> by someone else's.

I rise up out of the realms of dreams
to take a pee;
I do not merely get out of bed
but remain a perfect fusion of body
and soul. Dreams are the gifts given
to the living. I never take one
for granted. When my dreams die
I die.

Reality
     for Emily Dickinson
I bore reality through the night
and forged ahead with care.
To my astonishment, he emerged
none the worse for wear.
I held him tightly to my chest
reassured, and bolder
We gazed upon the rising sun
together one day older!

           I envy what the dead know
           but I can wait to find out.

Rex Sexton

Rex Sexton is a Surrealist painter based in Philadelphia and Chicago and his writing has that illusory element to it. His latest book of stories and poems "Night Without Stars" received 5 stars from ForeWord Clarion Reviews, who commented on the "wild beauty" and "joy of this collection ... the prose rabid, people hustling to survive their circumstances". Another collection of stories and poems, "The Time Hotel", was described by Kirkus Discoveries as "a deeply thought-provoking ... compelling reading experience." His novel "Desert Flower" was called " innovative and original" by Large Print Review, and, in a Kirkus review, "so skillfully devious it could have been written by Heinrich von Kleist two centuries ago in Germany". His short story "Holy Night" received the Editor's Choice Award in the Eric Hoffer Award competition and was published in Best New Writing 2007. His poems have been published in reviews such as bear creek haiku, Mobius, The Poetry Magazine, Willow Review and Edge. His book of artwork, stories and poems "X Ray Eyes" received acclaim by Chicago Art Magazine: "Sexton's work ... brings to mind the flattened forms and spaces and line qualities of Miro" ... the bizarre figures and spaces of Chagall ... bridging reality and fantasy through vaguely chimera-like figures/personified animals, and oddly flat ... pictorial spaces, Sexton's paintings emotionally engage viewers directly with multitudes of figures and multitudes of vivid expressions." He is married to neuroscientist Dr. Rochelle S. Cohen.

life's weary wander –
a white road lost

LIFE NOIR
Unknown hours fade to black.

DEATH OF A SALESMAN
Back and forth bats fly in the window.
Under the bed strange things hide and cackle.
A psycho's eye peeks my keyhole. I hope the
motel clerk remembers my wakeup call.

DO YOU STOP
at the red light in the dead
of night on the lonely street
where the winds howl and
shadows creep?

SUNRISE
Each day clouds race across the sky, a joy,
and at night, as you close your eyes to dream,
stars fill the sky, a delight. In between is the
feast of life: love, friendship, wondering, all
yours, everyone's, and all for the savoring.

Ed Markowski

Ed Markowski lives and writes in Auburn Hills, Michigan. Ed's short stories can be read in Smokebox Magazine.

county fair
the way the bearded lady
moves her hips

collision shop
a phone book turned to
divorce lawyers

zen garden
the symmetry
of cat prints

still
inside this album jacket
the
crisp brown husk
of
an ancient roach

loser's side
the weight
of the gatorade bucket

editing a poem
               snowflakes melt
                 on the salted blacktop

at the exit ramp...a roadside memorial

seedy motel
          a gideon's bible
          in mint condition

second honeymoon
our newlywed daughter
calls to check on us

anniversary dinner
we opt for
the tenderloin

Sean Perkins

Sean Perkins was born in Adele, Kentucky in 1966. His family moved to central Tennessee in 1976, and he has lived there since then. He gained his Bachelor's degree in English at Middle Tennessee State University in 1988, and he currently owns a cleaning service near Murfreesboro while teaching Yang taiji quan in the spare time.

Through bright, sweat-squeezing heat
Just above the asphalt,
A sparrow soars.

this violet air . . .
    sin of a thousand evenings
        empty

GENTLE RAIN: BEYOND HAIKU
The gentle rain falls
in the winter afternoon
on the grey-headed squirrel.

        soft, scented woman, please
          shatter me gently

(Sean Perkins, continued)

her midnight eyes,
    flash of
        some older, darker thing

                                faces
                                lost behind
                                yours

beyond the eyes and the hands and the voice
    just
        this

GENTLE RAIN: BEYOND HAIKU

The gentle rain falls
in the winter afternoon
on the grey-headed squirrel.

another day
    drowned of the ten thousand things; the
        scent of us

50

Alan Catlin

Real Short Bio Warts and All

Childhood dreams: a strange kaleidoscope of Virgin Island storms, suburbia hysteria, breaking windows, plates, glass. Family weekend visits in the "Haunted Place", Pilgrim State. Youth in a place that is part Peyton Place, part "The Heart Death of the Universe." College escape to twilight zone place caught in time warp somewhere between Coolidge and Hoover. Dual major in English and Substance Abuse. Charter member of The Whole Sick Crew. Roommate becomes the senator, "Someone had to do it." Someone has to become the scribe. That would be the poet. Graduate Work another city. Unfinished and unsatisfactory. Continuing studies in service industry. "You can learn more in a minute about life with your head held in a toilet than you can in seven and half years of college classrooms." Bad jobs and bad dreams. Toxoplasmosis and turmoil. One more unforgettable visit to the "Haunted Place". Five Dead and One Maimed for Life by the Age of 29: the short story and the life. Bad jobs, bad karma, bad everything. Stories and poems in the wreckage after. Another bad job, the last one. Lots of poems. A wife, two children and three grandchildren, so far.

Lifeguard stand turned face down. No one is saved today.

Colored sand falling in an hourglass. A pyramid of dreams

In the pause

>   between
>   fluid air
>
>   and still water
>
>   spirit lamps light
>   the way down
>   disused paths

False dawn: Deer prints in the snow. No deer.

After the fire. First snow tainted by ash.

The Indecency of Dreaming
is not confined to the body
made naked by a displacement
of skin once removed and
reformed as the lips of clouds,
the breach of birth waves make
once a storm has started to recede.

Reading green tea leaves. A taste of Zen.

Robert D O'Rourke

In 86 years I've covered lots of ground -- sorta like the "stuff" horses leave on pavement and pasture 1) as a kid, a "soda jerk"& a "delivery boy" (on my bike) for a drug store 2) a "hitch" in the South Pacific in the Navy, WWII (aboard five different ships B-4 that war ended) 3) *30 years a teacher, counselor, school psychologist* 4) *married to a beautiful woman (both inside-outside) for 59 years B-4 her crossing over to a better world - four kids result of that union* 5) *40 years a woodcarver of Santos - a meditative hobby* 6) *at present, retired: sometimes writer - volunteer @ Sr Center and Good Samaritan Nursing Home and Library ... a daily meditator attempting to be awake, living moment- to-moment, compassionate along my journey - enjoying my life with two cats, one dog and solitude*

sitting still
    among the rocks
        storms pass over

breathing deeply
    I fill my soul
        with Autumn

                caught
            in a spider's web floating
                summer moon

sometimes
the muses
are silent___
then
a flower blooms

winter
drifting in silent
soft snow

little pine tree
clinging to the
p
  r
    e
      c
        i
          p
           i
             c
               e

War
nothing beautiful
remains

Carl Mayfield

Began writing poetry about 40 years ago because I found some paper without any writing on it. Since the poem is never the thing itself, nothing that I write is what I wanted. For me, engagement with this life needs a poem now and then. The way I write is simple: if it's not true for one, it's true for none. As a side note, I have managed to stay out of jail for the most part.

End of day
   light fading . . .
my shoes still untied

  Wife's knees
        spooned into mine. . . .
  sound of the house doing nothing

kicking a stone by the mailbox − −
     patiently waiting
       for a reply

Only witness
to behind the knees kisses −
   the scented candle

What I wanted –
Well, dust is quick
to forget the busyness.

Blank look #101

            Enough with the wind
            if it can be moved
            it was in the wrong place

    thin line of geese
    the sky closing behind them

leaving room
on the couch
after burying the cat

her light kiss
lingering
        where it's needed

with her bra
around my neck
let winter come

56

Don Wentworth

Don Wentworth is a Pittsburgh-based poet whose work reflects his interest in the revelatory nature of brief, haiku-like moments in everyday life. His poetry has appeared in Modern Haiku, bottle rockets, bear creek haiku and Rolling Stone, as well as a number of anthologies. His first full-length collection, Past All Traps, was shortlisted for the Haiku Foundation Touchstone Distinguished Book Awards for 2011 and was published by Six Gallery Press.

Nest-Building

The list of a morning songbird
threads light into the weave
of night.

November Man

Second story window sill -
carton of milk, half a
sandwich - a hand

Sounds of Love

Your lips - a droplet of water
on a branch, the surface
off a pond.

attending to the fallen
         leaves
                  old priest and his rake

Issa's Answer
    The whole world sloughs off
    it's skin - do you have a question
    for Mr. Snake?

                  sitting straight - Crow knows

All my little legs

waving in the air, &

yes, your little legs , too.

LONG AFTER ISSA
Watch out, ants -
a clumsy sinner,
with big feet!

John Berbrich

John Berbrich was born and raised on Long Island, New York. He has worked in factories, a car wash, food service, and as a construction grunt - has played in several experimental rock bands, and is currently employed as an obscure paperwork drudge in a dreary government office building. He and his wife Nancy are co-rulers of BoneWorld Publishing, under the aegis of which are published the literary quarterly Barbaric Yawp and the many chapbooks of Muscle-Head Press. He writes monthly music & literary review columns for Fourth Coast Entertainment Magazine and is a founding member of SLAP (St. Lawrence Area Poets). John and Nancy live among the northwestern foothills of the Adirondack Mountains in Russell, New York.

We give it wide birth;
skunk in the road, flat as paper . . .
the smell . . .

Barefoot, I step outside
onto the cat's latest gift
a cold mouse-head

Quiet night walk
across the river
laughter and party-music

Nancy Berbrich

Born and raised in St. Lawrence County, Nancy Berbrich has been co-editor and co-publisher of the literary quarterly, Barbaric Yawp, and for MuscleHead Press, the chapbook division of BoneWorld Publishing, for the past thirteen years. She is one of the founding members of SLAP (St. Lawrence Area Poets), a local group of writers who seek to support and promote poetry in the North Country. Her poems have been featured in numerous magazines. She's been a teacher in the English and Communication Department at SUNY Potsdam for the past fifteen years. You can catch her as Spice on the Saturday morning radio show, Howie and the Wolfman on WTSC 91.1 FM here in Potsdam.

four wet dog noses
pressed on a frog in the road
wow! -- five spring away

Jody Bird Lawton

Born in Richmond, VA, 7/7/53 to George H and Mary Alice Bird, who taught me love of poetry, sent me to college and provided sound literary advice. A graduate of Forest View Elementary School, due to father's job, we moved to Bermuda where I attended Kindley AFB Junior High and High School. After much worldwide travel, I lived in my grandparent's hometown, Tucson, graduated from Tucson High School and the University of Arizona with a Creative Writing and English Lit BA. My work has appeared in bear creek haiku, Beginnings, Bell's Letters, Poet, Smile, Silver Wings, Haiku Hippodrome, Yasou, Coffee Ground Breakfast, Pancakes in Heaven, RB's Poets Viewpoint, Noble House and Iliad Press/Cader Publishing Anthologies, JMP Seasons of Change and Poets of the New Millennium chapbooks, J Mark Treasured Short Poems of 2001 Anthology, Poetry.com Sound of Poetry Series, and many other fine places. Among recent awards are Bell's Letters Poet First Prize Carrie Quick Award Fall 2012, Pancakes in Heaven God's Gift of Life Contest and their chapbook God's Gift of Life Oct. 2012, Smile Poetry Contest Spring 2012 and the National Silver Wings Poetry Contest 2011.

Yellow autumn woods
small purple insects come here
and laugh

Yellow petals lie
at the foot of the trees
like the shock of a lost hope
while we rush forward –
stories to time in
the damp wind.
The songs of the turtledoves
mourn for the lost horizon
of this cloudy day.

    February
pyracantha and bougainvillea
    bloom together

remember me in
Summer when green wordless songs
dance in the mind

stumbling on my walk
roots obtrude from warm concrete
autumn advances

Sharon Anderson

*a member of Greensburg Writers and Ligonier Valley Writers.
She lives in the historic village of Hopwood, in a stone house
surrounded by woods and wildlife. She is a freelance
designer and poet and has been published in many literary
journals, including, Lucidity, Black Moon, bear creek haiku,
Darkling, The Aurorean and Loyalhanna Review.*

This cement highway
I knew it as a dirt road
Born of a meadow.

conjugated
human being
  humans being
    human beings being. . .

    gone to find alice
    in the wonderland of heroin
    that endless rabbit hole and
    home to the junkie - maddest hatter of all

Statue in the park
Ulysses Grant on horseback
More polished in stone.

63

Brief Encounter
She dances alone
grasping her Southern Comfort
in a crowded bar
His picture phone rings
rousing him from a daydream
he whispers her name.

Raiment
One
man
clothed
in
Character
is
worth
two
in
Armani

traffic jam
a web of destinations
punctuality thwarted

Michael Ceraolo

a longtime contributor, lives in Ohio

Cleveland Haiku
The old ethnic dance hall
now the home
of the new ethnic poetry

suicide mission
buds blooming
before the last frost

A plaque
to honor its planting
the tree by itself inadequate

At the Coast Guard station
they wait and wait
for Canada to invade

Summer in the city –
ozone layer lolling
on the ground

(Michael Ceraolo, continued)

Cleveland Haiku
        265
Winter thaw —
ice sculptures
sacked by barbarians

        BASEBALL HAIKU

Baseball fight —
showing why
none of them box

        No bad seats:
        false advertising

Stadium shakedown —
a crime when committed
by anyone else

Growing up in Cleveland —
empty seats outnumber fans
ten to one

Vivian Bolland Schroeder

at home now in Crosby, Texas, her poetry over the past twenty years has been in numerous publications. Her three books of poetry, BUTTERFLIES AND WILL SWITCHES; THIS, TOO IS LOVE; and, CAMELLIAS AND CANNONS are available from the poet. An octogenarian, she completed her English BA in 1992 after six children and two resident grandchildren had flown the coop and her husband had retired from Boeing Company and NASA. She currently serves as caregiver, housewife, yardman, and mosquito buffet.

A bonus to rest:
Without structural changes,
Legs fold to form laps.

In absentia
Loved unconditionally:
Distant grandchildren.

HAIKU: FAMILY REUNION
Of more interest
than how she's kin, is her way
With blueberry pie.

SIGNING

Their joy contagious,
Smiles deepen and fingers fly:
the hymn-signing choir.

Will tomorrow's world
Recall nostalgically
Grandma's computer?

AFTER A YEAR AND A HALF OF THERAPY
you ask yourself,
if I don't love the darn thing,
who will?

Harbingers of spring:
Birdsongs, housecleaning frenzy,
Your bright yellow dress.

Filed among receipts
The warm smile of a shop clerk
In a tourist town.

Norm Davis

a retired school psychologist, Norm is the publisher and editor of HazMat Review, Rochester's premier literary journal. He is also the co-host of Writers & Books Wide Open Mike, and, the Pure Kona Poetry Series. Norm's poetry and other writings have appeared in many local and national publications, he is the author of one chapbook, Rome Gothic.

My father
always told me I
wouldn't amount to anything. But I
never got that far.

You know you are o-
verweight when you step on your
cat's tail, and it dies.

if you

build a better mousetrap
god (she's watching...
yes she is) will build a
better mouse

Three Cross Pass in Utah
we crawl through a muddy wet desert
water runs down to flood creek below
three crosses shiver on a small rise
conductor tells us the rain plays havoc
with the railroad signals system
I see five antelope with white behinds
their signal system not much
hampered by weather

after the poetry reading
we discuss how not to
make the same mistakes again

Poetry 2000's

We have
too few Lorcas
and way too many
Laureates.

70

poetry from three of our harbingers - - -

Denver Stull

> on strong north winds
> one last monarch
> fluttering north

Dave Church

> Bluebird on dead limb
> warbling
> "Ber-muda, Ber-muda"

and Giovanni Malito

> on the lake
> listening to the loon
> after it's gone

ayaz daryl nielsen ... husband, father, veteran, x-roughneck (as on oil rigs), x-hospice nurse, editor bear creek haiku (22+ years and 114+ issues) ... homes for poems include Lilliput Review, Shemom, Shamrock, Lalitamba, Lynx, various anthologies/awards (all deeply embraced), collections include Concentric Penumbra's of the Heart, and, Tumbleweeds Still Tumbling (all in the fierce wicked funhouse of poetry), beloved wife Judith Partin-Nielsen, able assistant Frosty, and! bearcreekhaiku.blogspot.com (translates as joie de vivre)

Peregrine

Your yearning is a peregrine
seeking, lost, and sought
From within your heart
exquisite longing raises
lithe wings into terrains of
emptiness, of divine rights
melting into blood and
passions, melting into holy
mischiefs within the fierce
wicked funhouse of poetry.

people pass by
  the dog
    waiting for dog

text sets - chalkduster *and helvetica*

bear creek haiku
po box 3787
boulder, colorado 80307 USA
darylayaz@me.com
bearcreekhaiku.blogspot.com
all rights reserved

5691028R00050

Made in the USA
San Bernardino, CA
17 November 2013